Priscilla Play

by

Tammy Raden

AuthorHouse™
1663 Liberty Drive
Bloomington, IN 47403
www.authorhouse.com
Phone: 833-262-8899

Because of the dynamic nature of the Internet, any web addresses or links contained in this book may have changed
since publication and may no longer be valid. The views expressed in this work are solely those of the author and do not
necessarily reflect the views of the publisher, and the publisher hereby disclaims any responsibility for them.

Any people depicted in stock imagery provided by Getty Images are models,
and such images are being used for illustrative purposes only.
Certain stock imagery © Getty Images.

This book is printed on acid-free paper.

ISBN: 978-1-4520-0808-0 (sc)

Library of Congress Control Number: 2010907213

Print information available on the last page.

Published by AuthorHouse   06/11/2021

authorHOUSE®

To Colby, Alexie, and Zachary,
who are the love of my life
and the inspiration behind all my stories.

The name of this girl is Priscilla Play.
She needs your help getting dressed today.
So gather her outfits and Priscilla too.
Then you dress Priscilla as I read this to you.

Now look for the dress that is black and red.
Then find the red bow that goes on her head.
Now socks and shoes is all she'll need
to leave for school where she can read.

Priscilla is ready, and she looks great
and because you helped she won't be late.
Wasn't that a lot of fun?
And we have only just begun.

The school day was fun and she learned a bunch,
but now she is home and ready for lunch.
But before she eats and playtime begins,
she needs your help getting dressed again.

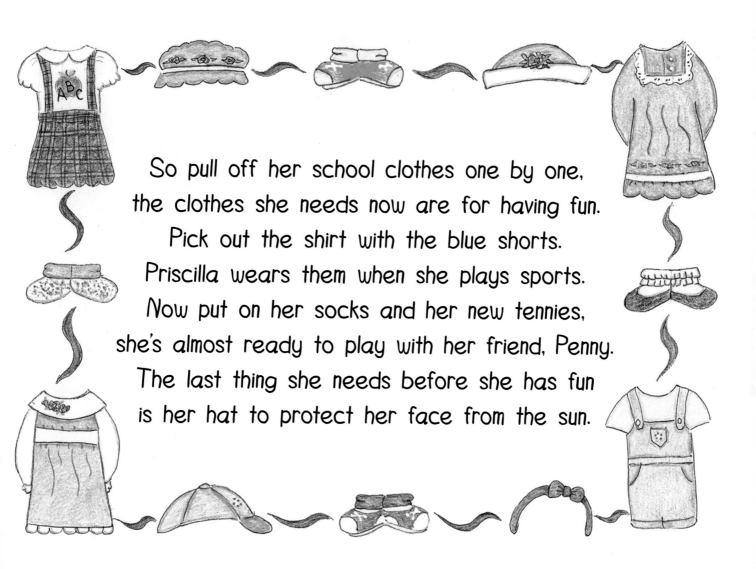

So pull off her school clothes one by one,
the clothes she needs now are for having fun.
Pick out the shirt with the blue shorts.
Priscilla wears them when she plays sports.
Now put on her socks and her new tennies,
she's almost ready to play with her friend, Penny.
The last thing she needs before she has fun
is her hat to protect her face from the sun.

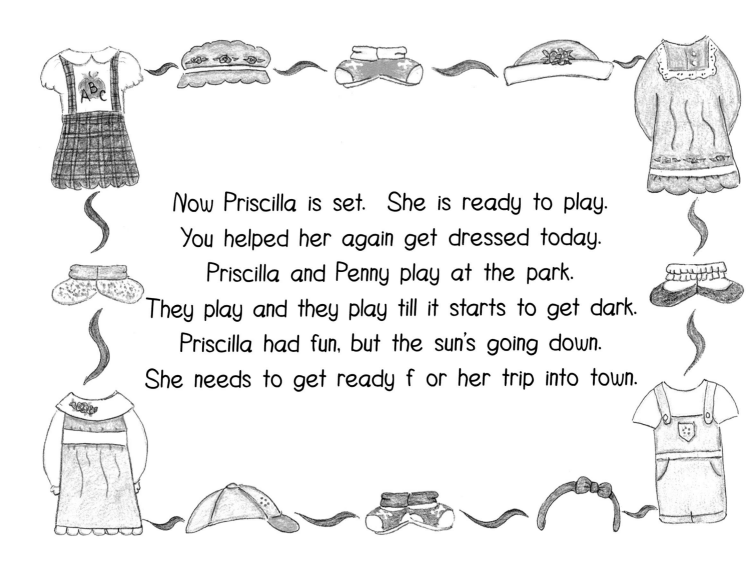

Now Priscilla is set. She is ready to play.
You helped her again get dressed today.
Priscilla and Penny play at the park.
They play and they play till it starts to get dark.
Priscilla had fun, but the sun's going down.
She needs to get ready f or her trip into town.

Penny picks up the ball and waves to her friend.
She knows that she'll see Priscilla again.
Priscilla must leave so she won't be late,
for tonight she has a special date.
Grandma and Grandpa are coming tonight
so she wants to make sure she looks just right.

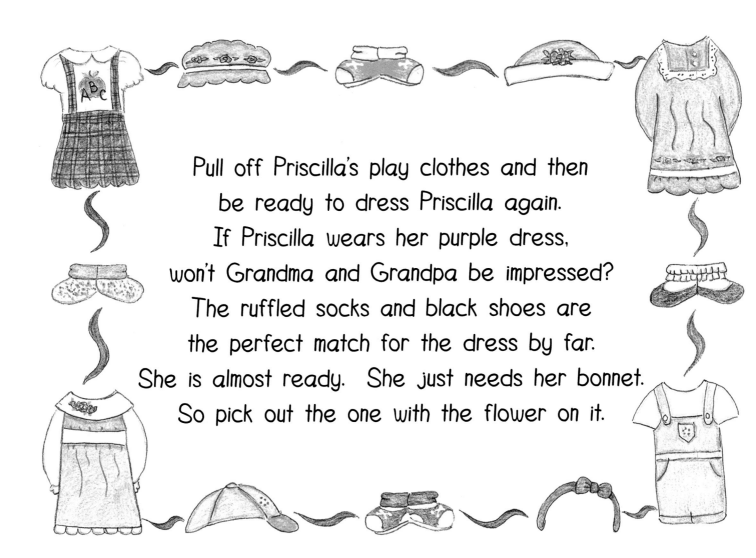

Pull off Priscilla's play clothes and then
be ready to dress Priscilla again.
If Priscilla wears her purple dress,
won't Grandma and Grandpa be impressed?
The ruffled socks and black shoes are
the perfect match for the dress by far.
She is almost ready. She just needs her bonnet.
So pick out the one with the flower on it.

Priscilla looks great. She's ready to go.
Because of your help, she's set for the show.
The show they are seeing is her favorite tale
of a princess and a prince she knows quiet well.
And when the show ended, it was almost eight.
They hurried home so they wouldn't be late.
Now let's help Priscilla one more time
to make sure she gets into bed by nine.

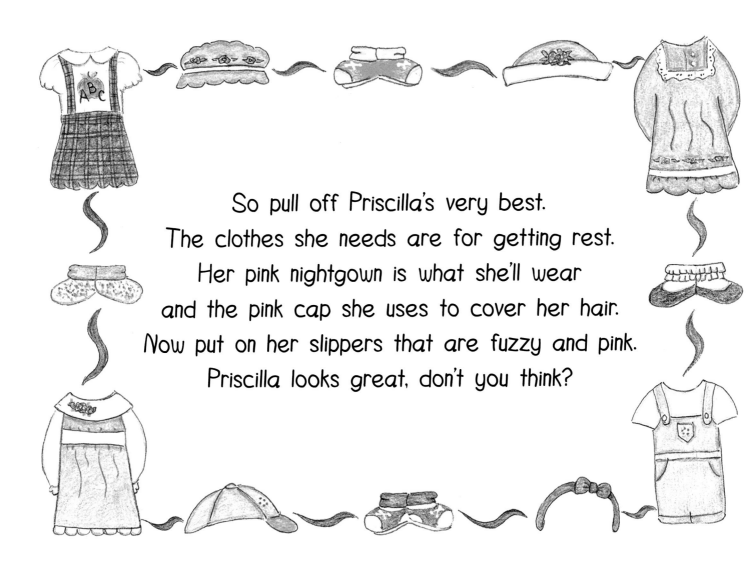

So pull off Priscilla's very best.
The clothes she needs are for getting rest.
Her pink nightgown is what she'll wear
and the pink cap she uses to cover her hair.
Now put on her slippers that are fuzzy and pink.
Priscilla looks great, don't you think?

Priscilla had fun getting dressed with you
but now she is tired, her day is through.
Before she sleeps she wanted to say,
"Thank you for helping me get dressed today."

Printed in the United States
by Baker & Taylor Publisher Services